Faulkner's Rosary

poems by Sarah Vap

saturnalia books

Saturnalia Books
105 Woodside Rd.
Ardmore, PA 19003
info@saturnaliabooks.com

ISBN: 978-0-9818591-6-3
Library of Congress Control Number: 2010934203

Book Design by Saturnalia Books
Printing by Westcan Printing Group, Canada

Cover Art: Codex Borbonicus 12
With permission of Bibliotheque de l'Assemblée Nationale: Paris, France

Distributed by:
University Press of New England
1 Court Street
Lebanon, NH 03766
800-421-1561

I would like to thank the editors of the following publications, in which some of these poems first appeared, sometimes in different form, or under a different title:

Blackbird, Ensemble Jourine, Gulf Coast, Hayden's Ferry Review, Listenlight, LOCUSPOINT, Merge Poetry Magazine, Natural Bridge, Puerto del Sol, The Laurel Review, The Journal.

Love and deep gratitude to Cynthia Hogue, Beckian Fritz Goldberg, Greg Donovan, Arielle Greenberg, Henry Israeli, Sean Nevin, Henry Quintero, Jessica Burnquist, Eva Valencia, Elizabeth Weld, Diana Park, Josh Rathkamp, Jen Currin, Mary Kay Zeeb, Jenny Browne, & Katrina Roberts.

Thank you, Lindy Fredson, for being with the children while I wrote.

Norman, thank you, and my abiding, joyful love.

Oskar, sweet boy, for your special role in this.

How to say it? Todd, Oskar, Mateo.

Table of Contents

For my beloved parents

What can we do with the shadow of a star,
When the star itself has bent its knees?

— Francis Ponge

Lifted adoring — then —

This is not the story of water, deadlocked,
or everblue — but a simple,

animal-faith breathing
not less

and not less.   The ducks in winter. Beaks
tucked to the saltwater that is thick,

now, with the estuary's mud. My mother

has gathered this water
in cream cans, wrapped the tub in towels

while we dye the chicks pink, blue,
and green for Easter — and our humanity

is not diminished. Coumadin

turns my father purple. He sits in a child's
wooden chair while my nephew hits him —

it is snowing.

This is just what I wanted. And hold
my father's beautiful face in my hands.

Linea Nigra: cross of jubilee

My *innermost* is a circle

holding your belly, the size
of a grain of rice.

My innermost is a wild upland,
and the piddling backwater of your father's

and my
libertinage. Star, I'm lit by the foxfire

of your very nub.

The blue braids in your baby blanket
are from the trousers of a state-trooper;

the blue tint of my labia
is the slip of a man.   My broad

and round ligaments
would tie chicken feathers

to the thoraxes of bees and follow
them back to their hive

where the weight of you—that's our each-other.

My world is sunlight.   Your world
is a single wave wrapped around.

Assembling
within me, our slightest idea

turned into roselight and chained

behind the sternum.

2

Someone to be good in front of

The older we are the more secrets

we are given to refuse—

I understood this the night we began.

As I now understand the nurse-cells
for your baby sperm.   And that testicles,

they help us; they will drag

a human soul out.

On the night of conception

we scattered the wasps in batches
to the alfalfa: eggs

in straight white rows
like braille on squares of black paper.

The wasps were to kill the caterpillars
who'd eat the sprouts.

Just now the baby moves

like coiling snakes—burst—

toward the peel of sunlight remembered

through my skin.

Memorare

She who knew what a body was

and gave him one, help me to distinguish
mouth from cock.   Help me to distinguish

the son from the mother: redeemer and
redeemed. It's simple to give glory be to the father, to the son, and to the holy ghost,

as-it-was-in-the-beginning-is-now-and-ever-shall-be-world-without-end-amen. But you,

throw the counterweight. You, window ajar. You, the floors swept

daily. You did make love and you did

dive deep into ourselves

within ourselves. At the beginning or near
the beginning. You, the true begin,

haven't I been faithful?

Conception

Haloes in children's drawings—the double-gravity

of light and homeland.
It's true

in the rhubarb patch behind our home—licking the ends,
dipping them into sugar,

chewing and spitting out the pith—that's

the way children are. Resting alone in the tin shed, resting inside

the enormous wall
of the white lilac bush.   I had my proof, like growing hair,

that there's nothing to do about the dailiness
of intimacy.   Freshborn animals—

the parsley smell of their afterbirth,
and my first-dream of the lightning that ricochets

between two blue glaciers—these became the questions of deserving
or demanding

a lover who refers to me as *Luxury*—

but won't sleep along me. Not tonight
while we call you toward us.   Calling to you

since I, myself, was the child.

Arizona

He knows that there are two beings in a door, that the door awakens in us a two-way dream

On the trip: two shooting stars

out the car window. Two washes of electricity
through my whole body

in the hours after we'd made love.   I knew there were two
and I wanted—wanted

to start over. To remake myself against these rocks. Against children
that I would curl my bones around: pits

so solid in the center of me
I'd be held outright like a star. Wanted to dash myself, as women do,

against the infants. Wanted

over hours of washboard road
to the edge of the canyon. And there,

wanted the whole hollow. I wanted the edge.

Wanted the drop, the curved drop. I wanted a ghost. My belly
a long time on the hot ledge: rock,

then skin, then figment. Figment,
then spine, then sky.   The river's blue spine

was miles below—I whispered *stay*
and I told you: *two.*   I closed the book on your lap

and opened it to the word: *double.* I closed the book
and opened it: *twice.*   When we arrived at our next stop—

the meteor's landing in the desert—though we searched

down the play of our family; searched
the old mother with the child stuffed

back into her body; searched prehistory's foil balloons,

failing lights, and volunteers who told us where
exactly—exactly—

to step—we found
only a single crater to once shatter earth. We found only

one task of explosion,

and only the sun for its lamp.

Eggtooth

As I wanted, when a girl, my grandmother's clay beads. Vinegar
into the dye and the rosary—my Easter necklace—

green as the spring needles. My grandmother

making the braided bread. Singing
the leaping song of the gazelle in the marriage vow:

I wanted you, baby, braided,

braiding though me, even then. Wanted you
pulling at the wheat's

seed-fold while she sang to spring and simultaneous:
your father.   Somewhere else in the world

just a baby. Your father cooing—cooed

to my hands, like a clock—   right then.

Right then, is when you came.

Children

In us recurrences.

When, beyond the patience of night's long black grass,

they're locked into that shape
of the small white chastity—it's hardly this simple—

of their basic cells. Link to link;

counting prayers to recall what their bodies should be.

There is an Ave; there is a rose;

there is a son: this low chanting.

This small hum this calling to life
through night which covers the face—it's

winterpond's peaceful dose of sleep, and below that water,
Faulkner's rosary—

father son father

mother son mother—. It's what their hearts hold

that becomes truth,
as far as we know truth.

We grew in a redwood house

Everybody knows why the dragonfly's
spoon-shaped penis scoops

the rival sperm out.

Who'd question the dragonfly unless to prove
that the natural world is broken

in this scared little girl with nicknames like devil's
darning needle, horse-killer,

eye-pisser and ear-stick. She'll sew your lips together

or worse. Girl
with knotted hair—and black grass teeth.

Her mind-of-night creeps

toward the relays of blue light
frozen over the pond at sunrise—

I keep thinking you'll tell us a secret: as blue wings of tiny

latched-together dragonflies. *He'll pierce*

the female's head with his pincers
to hold at her while she flies

to make the babies with patinas
like the ice.   The babies' bodies determined,

the pond will redden with them by summer.

Fallopian

I don't know what it was like for you,
before me.   Wrapped-up, did your night

walk with you? And practice speaking

like the black rock
slipped secretly, hand to hand, by a new love

to a new love? Then, is forever looked-after?
Welcoming,

and not very happy, the black cat
turns into a white one

as it crosses the stone wall of the Street of the Holy Spirit.
Something untouchable, we know,

is still voluble.

A cradle of warmed oats for the chickens on the Epiphany

Last week you formed the chambers of your own heart; this week
the lobes of your brain. I wake up thinking *overcelebrate*.

I wake with the phrase *as I am wont*.

Chronology doesn't enter—my birth and yours,

my mother's pregnancy
and mine, they are the same: blessed,

and tendered thanks for infinite detail—windowsills,

before or after Advent, where the worm lived

by your vanished sister. You must dream

of animals, afraid,
pitching themselves

into hollowed-out buildings, built

several stories down into the earth.

Meditation on pink

The icy drink, the umbrella. Delicacy
of accepting on faith … accepting that I am

and I am not your whole horizon: I'm waiting for what binds
things together—what's not arbitrary

of pink icing. Rose fabric
to cover the chair; the fringe of my girlish

blanket when I still viewed myself as very far away,

not very far inside. But the pinks don't hold. Water jugs, lip gloss,

wildflower. Swirl in the floorboards. Swirl in the sunset, pink
baby-finger or threads of milk

from the nettles,
from here dripping into evening's long

taproot. Twilight, the shape of on oyster over the backyard,

darkens the ruffled

summer dress at night's pink impasse.

Meditation on blue

Dawn's stooped cornflower next to my grandmother's
blue glass salt

and pepper shakers; her brooch's indigo stone
each dazzling morning—

no one recognizes
morning's desperation— the inattention

that ended here, I thought,

with love. Your shoulder....sky.
Taking off my shoes—this happiness?

Heavy glass door for your gracious

and casual dismissals of my memory:
boiled eggs for Easter on our stove's flame—and every so often

some morning star,   or some past voice.

Trusting being hooked to your life—where worlds break apart,
then freeze together: I've done

everything you told me to do.

Living together

One'll make it so the other
can grow rapt—in your slippers,

you're a starlet dancing

each morning.   If we'd been bare outside
we'd have heard whole stars

with our whole body. Appliqué—day

onto night. I can tell when a day'll
be brutal, when a lap-

dance will make me laugh at morning.

And when I'm tired of myself, I will love
your morning's confidence.   Your capable,

ornamenting hands—. Adding

one to another—stringing

over and over, your welcomes.

It never hurts immediately, father. Or son. Or holy spirit.
As I was in the beginning, nests and shells, and ever shall be. World, still hidden, amen.

Howling cabooses alongside

If we're redoing being loved. Dragging

our feet to stop a life with our efforts
at deep familiarity.   Magpies and blue jays

fight at the basin of nuts
we put out for Christmas, too high for the bears.

Expressiveness, I tell you,
of your beard: hairless when you're trustful.

Bearded quickly when I flail—or, am ruined
         by not making it into your dream. We're envoys

to one another's quietest life,   where we're beholden

then unbeholden.

A bear as big as an angus in my parents' backyard

The wolf is in the front, his back above the alfalfa.
Between them, the parsing house,

and the patch of wildflowers my father planted from seed that spring.

Mother holds the bull-trout from hip to ankle. Her pole
has frozen to the lake.   When I was a child we mistook

baby bears for dogs until they loped—she tied the bear-bells to our jeans,

called our dog for its warning-smell, then sent us out to play.

Children's drowning-stories each spring—snow

from the mountains into the drainage creek. A quarrel
with life—certain lives do that—

if it's a mountain lion, look bigger.
          Their operative lop-lops—quietly the child
who lags.

If it's a grizzly—back away and be silent,
fold beneath your pack.

My parents' farm was called Beargrass. Our dog was named Bear.

Avoid their berry patches,   cow-parsnip thickets
and fields of glacier lily.

The river is wiggle-room between wildfires.

If I drown in our rivermouth,

in its bed of glacial milk—you're responsible for yourself. *Don't eat before you swim*

because the lurching-gait of hypothermia

will turn the picnic like the giardia.

A kingdom of garish cat's-eyes

Remember smashing fireflies to our ringfingers
then playing married? Our diamonds

glowed past bedtime. Remember

dying the pigs' tails
like the eggs—

Lullaby for a disappearing child

We're thankful for

this new day's morning-bird. Its piece of lace
and a shy look west through the canyon.

This day's beak.   Thankful for my new day's

anxiety: sunlight asleep in bed with you, cat with me,

our grape juice
spilled by the dresser.   Grateful patio door open—

at last, bearable
winter in the desert, filled with the birds

that are only pretty in the snow.

Seem dying in this pink sand.

We consider the bird left behind. Consider
birds at night—

tall thin birds. And the gems,

thickly like bells.

Spill

When icebergs rode in on great floods, then out again
with great emptying—

that bottleneck of mountain and ice
held a lake over my hometown: when I think of children

I think of the children there. Children
who prayed with me all those years at the church school.

When I think of children I think of us gathered

at the cement statue of Mary,
up in the tree in May. We'd dress her in white,

we'd crown her with flowers, and carry her
inside to chant   *mystery to mystery*

along the church walls. The deepest point of the lake,

I knew, must have rested
at those walls.   When the neck melted

the whole lake rushed
back to the nurseries of the ocean, but my daughter

is stuck at the mouth. Satellite, comet, diamond

make it out there
into the ocean—jellies

stars daughters—but the actual baby? Mystery, sorrowful. Mystery,

magnificat—as the lake that simply warmed

and then was completely lost.

Moonlight and firelight, beholden to the desert

You wake me to remind me of the icetruck
through the canyons to Phoenix.   Remind me of my morningtime

faithfulness… bent on snow.
All my goodness

kept in snow and firelight's meter. For one afternoon I watched the sunlight
trace a red cliff. That evening, a boy

dressed like a dragon

spit out a cloth flame at the grocery store, and we agreed: let's live
in a quieting house

lost in the snow

and warmed with that fire. Let's leave sunlight's heat,

these pinkish winters.

Summer: the pink fungus on rocks, wild raspberry, and pushed-mud dams

Yesteryear snows; diesel
in dad's heroic white truck—

our life in the Bitterroot Mountains.
Oh, bar-do! Oh, lim-bo! We're the last who'll see

wild animals and snow
to stifle the world for certain. The last children

who'll wade the mythic river to gather

planks for the driftwood mantelpiece
below our pitched cedar ceiling—

our hearth was found-quartz and creekstone

at the center of our long house
built along the mountain drainage—frozen,

like the tectonic ripple below.
The whole house frozen—history frozen to memory,

memory frozen to the solid rock
of summer. Summer, waiting and warming

each winter's

sweet lamb at its fold.

Sonogram

... don't suppose that fate's any more than childhood's density.

The bearded cloud—softest
possible for the baby blanket snapped out

before it's hung to dry.

In loop-de-loops the fog lifts
to reveal

our first white rainbow.

Hundreds of waterbirds, in exact-unison,
under its arc—

the real birds with their reflection dance
        for synchronized wintertime. The baby

under my heart watches me watch the rainbow,
watch the birds, and something in him must land, or

one bird fall back alone into the water, forgetting summer.

Identical to the memory

that sets the birds turning,
turning together over winter's bay

where my husband
swam his whole life. The birds split in two, and,

with the wind and their doubles, make
the flat blanket ovoid.

Sonogram

I have to trace water

all the way back: the air is for ideas.

The water is for feeling
the ocean's grandiloquent

belly-laugh—a geyser's
multiplying ropes shot

from the hip of rock. I watch
this blue light of us, creature, and I know,

I'd like us
to be the less delicate.

The humanity ghost

Our lilac bedsheet is the opposite of aggression.
Toward the sonogram's little

crocheted ear—his daydream

deepening to a dream
of the canyon's crosswise rib. We knew he had landed

inside me when we saw the meteor-crater

by the blue-green river—its orientation toward what is writ

in the stone. We have
to think of this hole

as better than the original star. Pronged
rubble indicates not two sides of a star, but one

violent circumstance that evolves

something for our whole life: an animal-filament.

Rattle a fat azure
feather, to bless what's pinned itself
inside us.

Glory be to the water, to the sun, and to the holy ghost.
As love was deepening, is now, and ever shall be—my world without end

in the arms of a curve. Amen.

Horizontal lightning

The sky is silver and red

above a dark that sags.

Flecks… broidery: the picnic tablecloth

gone onto the hillside. One baby safely
swaddled in his turquoise flannel.

The exemplary life

of the light, of light's
tentacle to the clock

high in the throat of the sun. Pity
is what's called forth

when we slide
back to the least vanished.

Sonogram

How to make sense of my hope: our eagerness
to speak for one another,

for our wishes. This is the catastrophe

of hope. The stranglehold of hope: I wish
that my life will be.

The sense of my life that will die,

if touched
(like some exotic waxrose)

by the oil of a human hand.

In the dream you were the horse

Is it simpler to say it like this: we waited
for that huge pattern of flocking birds, and then his lipping,

just barely tethered.

Sonogram

The girl is the color, you think, of electricity.
Children's energies like ballerinas

showing themselves off. Snow as high as me.
We complain about children sometimes because they take away

our ability to make
everything even. The testing-us remains—how to comfort

ourselves, alone,
when it's snowing peacefully

from morning until evening—even when I think I understand.

Undiminished,   the greatest woman
eventually pulls us all into herself. Snow wraps around her

like the long veil of cotton, smoothed
and smoothed.

Baby I want to give you something invisible you motherfucker

The mother to idealize

lives and loves

somewhere between Mary and Mary. I make her a dress.
It's beautiful, sheer.

Embedded in the dress is a poem.

To read it through the sunlight
I hold the dress to my kitchen-sink window, the hem

dips in the dishwater—women are ruined
buying expensive dresses. Red ones,

stretched to nudity.

The poem says I will not desert you in your trouble.

That it takes twelve dragonflies to subdue one hare

and you don't know
how your own hands slide

to flap

your own little wing-bones.

The last question of snow & childhood

Bright shock of desert summer—in stockyards, the goat

that leads the other animals to slaughter is the Judas—his bleats
I remember, begged

my palm for sugared peanuts
that night in the tornado shelter

when I asked my mother how to pray,

how go to heaven—.
I was kicked out of the gifted-program

for such sanctimoniousness.

But today, the trees where my family lives are crystal-feathered.

The whole valley crystal this way—the fawn and no fawn
in the snow-mist,

in the snow-wind and they are all in heaven.

The hummingbird's not yet

at the yellow tip of our aloe—
at our ease of hallucinating snow;

of adding to oneself all night long
until it's morning, it's the desert and very hot—

and grandfather's corn is in our cinnamon, in our milk.

The laundry carousel heats
our socks in the sunshine, heats our t-shirts and below it—

the quail, whose curled
headfeather is the delicate *why* bobbing

just above her whole life,

leads a row of eleven babies the size
of thumbs. Their own miniscule curls already lilting:

guess, guess. *Why the opposite of snow is moon?*

The moon last night, brightening
its own forgiving gaze.   My questions

of earning my salt slowly

by dancing slowly
for the player-piano on my 8th birthday. Dunk the new,

beautiful doll's white braid into the punch to brighten
what might be her simple

laborious life of love. The dark shells of the birthday necklace
crack one by one. Against the windowpane where a light,

almost solid, falls like fine needles

for testing the blood's
sugar. Then stays, like committing roses —

their white heat, to the ground.

Self-portrait as a butter-churner

—for your dream

Fungi-like white angels
with the dozen long clear wings

inside testicles, highly-magnified:
obstinate coils

with beaks like scythes—*sweet-cream butter, or salted*—
this is how I will know

if I can make a home. My great-grandmothers
in the Moravian salt marsh

gathered minerals

for their crystal mill—but was that enough to know
if they would lay down a burden

to pick up the more natural responsibility?

Linked pinkies,

the edges of our eyes close, open
like belts of wood beneath the cooper's

certain ascending and descending hoops—

mouthfuls at the crank of the barrel-churn, of sweet cream
before the butter arrives.

Snuggery

Long was I hugg'd close—long and long.

It's wooed; my little
hearth's invaded. That we were the least of them with helicopters

over our apartment every day—then the eviction,

the shittiest landlord. My lilac
summer dress in the car ride through the canyon—charged by the sunset's orange

to brown—I did feel the two babies then.
I feel one baby right now. In our new house, phosphorous on a match

to mask the previous renters' smells. Wash the curtains
of dog hair, wash the nest

from the disconsolate chimney. All my darling recombinations
waiting for their place

and I can't move for bedrest, *pelvic rest*—
to the mountain where I grew up. I mean that I can't go home.

Where ancient watermarks
wrap the low hills.

Where the lake was strapped

behind its glacial dam. Higher, the peaks where that glacier
once calved her bergs—lobes

spread down my parents' valley;

carved out my childhood's tributary. But that's too close

a parallel   fog, blessedly over that valley,

and this remaining baby.

Fink, Punk, Nincompoop, Honky-tonk, Sunlight, Sunnysideup, Ding-a-Ling, Tiger

Father sketched me pregnant; a light-blue dress
and the hem drags

like the giant
waste of morning sleepyheads, one after the other out of bed.

Simple memories: my father making pancakes.

New nicknames every morning...   Imposter, Gangster, Shaggy, & Hobo.
He told us about his unpreparedness to be the father

each day on the way to school. He'd say we owe it

to tempting providence. Understand, for my father,
lineage—what he'd be missing?: God, the Cloth, and his brothers' calling.

Not the priesthood, but *I believe in you*

and breadwin. Counterbalance of come-to-rescue:
father

is total ancestry—. Remember, for every baby born
there are countless playing dead.   Remember heraldry,

and his Gabriel-moment—I was fathered by the angel who tells
the story of a Victorian house, buried

underground.   It was built by aliens. It's fully intact.
It's discovered by his children.

To be breathed-in by a god

Enthusiasm is Greek
for *gods within*. My birthright is not a life in the desert canyon—

buttresses of pink stone
where we lift

sacrifice off. Freud says *uncanny*

to describe women's effect on men.   But the status of Mary's
unstable: Mary-mother-of-god, Mary Magdalene,

of Bethany, Kay, Quite
          Contrary. Women

strike bargains, the world over. Or perhaps

I could simply say this: I am not able to understand
myself.   And: we have lost

and we have lost the girl.

Glory be to the boneless, to the lipless, and to the breastless.
As she was in the beginning, is craved, and ever shall need. World without end. Amen.

Horses

The sonogram's heartbeat was like galloping hooves, a fireblue

light herding us
to true love. The second horse long gone.

When you say "pandemonium"

—the family's already arranged, and what we

have exchanged for a daughter—I love

the attention to my dress: bright red and quite pretty. Oyster-
shell pattern. Buttons

shaped like hibiscus, and very ushering.

By silence

The wanting you
was so much quieter than this. Quieter

than I know how to say. Once by fire. Once by water.

I wanted you by commotion. By the hem

of sunlight across your father's wrist. I wanted
you there, embroidered

to the curtain brushing his shoulder. There, his beard
where—he whispers, does he? *Io*. Io,

burning moon

the consistency of oil—most exploding

object in our solar system. We were led to you

by explosion, led to you
by the opening

and closing gesture of a bomb—flipping once—

to his neck, pushing

to the beard like the mother bird, he says, that will push

and turn. Turn to smooth

the walls of her nest
while she waits for the babies to break open. Circles

the home until her breast
is full of the green needles of spring: I want you there. Sharp

and new at the heart like that.

Pandemonium

Palace, cathedral: the thickening light in the heart of the house.

Tiny bug buried below the rock

or drawn like the moth

toward light?   Little daemon. Unfaithful
part of the house. What is the first thing

the house took. Upright spirit, pound the floors, .

pound the hearth, and who would save the house.

Who would kill the house

with a whisper inside the house. The slow and the detailed
thickening at the house. The house thickening

and the heat

thickening to ornate the house. Heat thickens
deep to the house.   Heat that would snarl the cathedral,

heat would wilderness

the steeple. Heat would break and rebuild
the whole hell, that held house.

Quickening

I anticipate, as stallions anticipate—our work.
Toward a horse-faced river, horseflies—or the sounds
of children at play

as countless horses in the river—

we both know
how to heed a calling. We both know

what patience is—it rips out your throat—.

Reconcile

The earliest light we know

is out there on the hill this evening, calling to us. Starlight

is an ancient lilac, a talent for the fragile certainty:

there is a speck
of memory. Then it is quiet.

It's sacrilege to imagine

how someone should or should not
have loved you, umpteenth time.

Primagravida

When the earth was young and exploding herself, did these
things happen then?   The fern coiled

into the ash where she will harden

for our understanding of time.   This desert holds time
so clearly: the standing-up rocks—

spires like stacked brown eggs—as if to prove time's

great preference for childhood.

When the tornado touched the frosted swingset
of my winter-evening birth, my mother told me—my crib

was borne from the bottom
of the pelican's beak.   With feathers

for pillows like pale, pale birthday tulips—

I was frightened— then cracked,

like my mother's twilight sleep.

Unloose

They say God himself engraved

the tablets for Moses: this law

might let impulse
disappear from the world

forever. In favor of

a never-moving pole:
a reindeer herd in the barn. Oh God,

Gentle Steward—

gather wildnesses

directly to this moon, ridden halter & leadline,

ridden bareback—*that* tame
moon circling

the one still spot. But we understand
how stewards can be—fumbling in secret

to make the contraption that would help the child

making the weary woman. Someone built

to hold or like the moon, to circle. Someone built

to simply tire, alongside.

Making love in the middle of May

Thistles grow below the pomegranate

outside our window; overhead,
the release of thatch from around itself—a rotted handful

where the brown spider has made her nest.

Our boy will sit on this mattress
to pick the stickers from his socks.

Maybe he's just walked through the alfalfa,

each step raising a spray of grasshoppers over his head.
Our girl might be like me. She will braid brown

and white threads for her bookmark. She will string
the beads that dangle from her hair,

that strap her wrists. The bead that sparkles her ear,
her hem, her cuff;   beads,

they told me when I was a girl, from across the world

where my grandmothers were born.

But right now,

how full I am. Our son and you are both inside me—
we three are in love, and our girl

is just a thought.   She's the hop,
flutter of a small

brown bird, then its leap to another branch
where the flutter is transferred to.   She is wisp and we

are very solid. Right now,

the rotating fan's a relief every few moments.
Assemblages of relief.

The shavings of relief when everything's good
in our docile house.

Inlaid

The dying he is about to do—being born
out of me—I feel him fasten, and refuse it.

There is almost everything

in the world in him—he is ready. His eyes, hooked to his face.
His arms to his body. His charity

is linked to his justice,

his warp to woof.   Detailed, he is thickened:
he has made himself

adorned of cells linking
the one to another. He is linked to himself, we have linked

each other we are linked

of him: the omphalos

teems. It will
detonate our Lent—the waiting season

that will unhook us from each other.

If I can name how gentle, we'll be that. If I could name when

if we could name
exactly who, this baby, his pieces all together, his bits

strung together, he'd maneuver—
genuflect—

and appear, wouldn't he, something else

and unraveled of me.

Call

I don't know seven rounds

of my maternal line—
Sarah, daughter of Linda,

daughter of Joan, daughter of Sarah,

daughter of Mary—tiny,
unornamented women. My women's catechism

is the plain string of beads for prayer, is the pew,

and the *pietà*: they took

one step toward love.

Love took the two steps toward me—marking
time in a crib of alfalfa.   The count

of days as love

accumulates: fattened
by this son I had to have, and cannot name.

Glory be to the cluster, and to the string, and to the holy spontaneity.
Intimacy in the beginning, is now, and ever dissolving. The world, without. Amen.

Phoenix spring sunshine

After morning it will be too hot, and after April—
walking in fire. I ask

that you forget

that where we live now, there are only birds in winter.
They'll leave soon for the northern

summer procession of dreamy, selfless x's.

Summer in Phoenix: an answer to the vanishing god

This morning, husband,

you lay beneath the window and dreamed of many people
watching you sleep through that window, while

this overdue boy is still

and quiet inside me, I tell you, like a dog who's snuck muddy onto the bed.
Hopes he won't be noticed so he can stay

a little while longer.
Now the halo is written within me, I wake with those words,

and to someone bucking hay within me—. My moon, full of mangers—
fontanel and temple—

red dome and below –

his delicate footing is the trace of two white kites.

Sunlight is orange through blood

The sun's light
will unthicken us. Will reach, even, the free grace

of this dark mover because God,
he knows, *cannot* go away.   This morning, our cat's

plump trot to the kitchen where together we sing, high-pitched and quickly,
tuna, tuna, tuna.

She will clean her face sitting on the kitchen table,
happy sister of light.   She will lift her black tail, so gently,

with her white paw to her tongue—full-complement
to our own son,

umbilical in his mouth, or yanked on like the miner's bucket.

He will pass
inside-out of me, so that it will become impossible to stand apart

from my lived-life. This morning

we hang mismatched dark sheets over our white curtains, wrap
the house's eyes to keep out the heat.

Our rotating fan will blow

over the bowl of ice, faithfully all afternoon. A blizzard's
copper orbit amidst this solar-happiness—

the hot sway of our domicile, rather than his dominion.

June

The rainbow ring from the prism in the window

moves across our kitchen wall. Onto this damn
lazy cat cleaning

from its bottom while the drunken couple dances

after Church on the Street.

When was it like that?   Dill and lemon, vegetables
clutched together beneath the rings of blue and orange and green

which move, finally,

along the string of tiny clay bells
we've hung as the welcome

over our door.

Fandango, triple-time

Is love
like baiting? Interested

until standoffish—consent
about how we'll let it look.

We're kissing each other. I know who wants
to look like the holder, and how

to make being held look

like holding something extraordinarily
ponderous.   Potency,

then impotency
of withholding my body—try

though I might.

Saint-star, itching-pea

The baby's ears drop between my hip-points.

My belly is a blood-vessel filigree. Stretched,

it looks draped
with bougainvillea: the baby is right there.

This living baby
is just beneath the memory

of my miscarriage cousins' graves —

marked with pinwheels so that even the wind

endures that sacrifice.　　The pinwheels' wind,

as if to answer this lament for my aunt,
lament for babies — whips out my dangling crystal earring

to sparkle by the grave. Spins the adoration song

that accompanies this offering

Apartment building named *Fontanel*

Giving you every reason in the book

to ask me nicely to go. Elbows into sides, all the night.

Move to the wall-side, please,
and stay. Digging myself holes.   Under carpet. Robbing Peter to pay—   stop

dickering. Hello! Hello, Prince.

The heartstone beads

Who in her dream could leave a child, isosceles

across his crib—he's the thinnish wedge of light

like flexible childhood love. He isn't born, but rolled up in the cave
at Nag Hammadi, and won't disturb the lambing ewe.

Will let her lick her babies clean. He won't force their mouths

to her—or their wooliness to the very
edge of collapse. That balance, that relay of wool just an instant in the life

of stone's pigment; or, the two-horned uterus

pushed out like a valentine.
There's the ritual of sweeping before stepping across a threshold;

but at night, don't sweep the ancestors'
welcome away. I'm doubling

and full of the prima materia, but my baby will cry in utero.

Maybe for his dream about caring for animals
as gently as if he were holding another person's body.

Maybe for my heartbeat...

the murmur. The blood's
regurgitation instead of booming song

about this blessing given to him:

a bracelet woven into the thunderbird...
on the left wing, night moves to daylight.

On the right, day towards night. When he is born

the scissortails will join

to latch these ends together.

Green moon

To be guardian of you,
as of myself... the greatest harm

is to mention everything, nervously.

We imagine breathing, and also, our undressing.
Sometimes, we might not know

what to send in place of ourselves, even though
people in a row, talking,

overlap with some
total lineage,

beating on our cloth doorplate.

Return, return, return (Jiménez); Contact! Contact! (Thoreau)

Our life is stilled.

Not stopped, and not
in peril. We bathe our cat

on the last full moon
of your gestation—we call this the midnight mass. Iris loves

her bath; purrs embarrassedly by the moon's limelight
on our white cactus flower—her beatification

in the summer dark. It's no longer painful; it's simply too long.

My desire for you is undesperate,
and yours for me.

We wait along with you—crushing peppermints

for the ice cream, describing for one another memories

of the curtain of rain—
a round, grainy night with your great-granny who wore her thimble out

every couple of years. And great-grandmother who wore
the artificial lilacs in her hair.   My women

my men
and childhoods are all within you—our body's the vise

and screen where you project
your beautiful dreaming. A dream to distinguish this calm

from the terror that is elaborate—

is cathedral. From our calm, intricate—as this wailing

mouth's rose.

Hail holy body, earthquake, and jaws. Hail banished children: look at us.

As in the beginning, we shall see him as he truly is.

After exile, O mercy, show us the womb.
O knife, O promise, O glory: it is not yet clear what we shall become. Amen.

Notes

Lifted—adoring then—: title from Dickinson
Someone to be good in front of: title from Elizabeth Weld
Arizona: epigraph from Bachelard
In us recurrences: epigraph from Rukeyser
We grew in a redwood house: some language from *National Geographic*,
    April 2006
Summer: the pink fungus on rocks: italics from Bachelard
Sonogram (p. 27): epigraph from Rilke
Baby I want to give you something invisible you motherfucker: title from
    Karen Finley & is for Mary Kay Zeeb
Last question of snow and childhood: for Diana Park
Snuggery: epigraph is Whitman
Sain star, itching pea: for Nancy
The heartstone beads: for Henry Quintero, for his gift to us

Cover: From the thirteenth trecena of the *Codex Borbonicus*, the Aztec
Sacred Calendar. The thirteenth trecena is under the auspices of
Tlazoltcotl, goddess of steam baths, midwives, cotton, weaving, filth, sex,
vice, prostitutes, adulterers, disease, and purification. She seduces and
inspires licentiousness, then forgives and purifies the adulterers by
absorbing the filth into herself. She is often portrayed with black around
her mouth and chin, wearing a conical hat, riding a broom, or squatting
in a birthing posture– the face of the emerging infant upside-down just
below her own. Of the cover image, what is not shown of the image is
Tlazolteotl giving birth to her son Cinteotl, god of maize.

Also Available from **saturnalia books**:

Personification by Margaret Ronda
Winner of the Saturnalia Books Poetry Prize 2008

Gurlesque: the new grrly, grotesque, burlesque poetics edited by Lara Glenum and
Arielle Greenberg

Tsim Tsum by Sabrina Orah Mark

Hush Sessions by Kristi Maxwell

To the Bone by Sebastian Agudelo
Winner of the Saturnalia Books Poetry Prize 2008

Days of Unwilling by Cal Bedient

Letters to Poets: Conversations about Poetics, Politics, and Community
edited by Jennifer Firestone and Dana Teen Lomax

Famous Last Words by Catherine Pierce
Winner of the Saturnalia Books Poetry Prize 2007

Dummy Fire by Sarah Vap
Winner of the Saturnalia Books Poetry Prize 2006

Correspondence by Kathleen Graber
Winner of the Saturnalia Books Poetry Prize 2005

The Babies by Sabrina Orah Mark
Winner of the Saturnalia Books Poetry Prize 2004

Velleity's Shade by Star Black / Artwork by Bill Knott
Artist/Poet Collaboration Series Number Six

Polytheogamy by Timothy Liu / Artwork by Greg Drasler
Artist/Poet Collaboration Series Number Five

Midnights by Jane Miller / Artwork by Beverly Pepper
Artist/Poet Collaboration Series Number Four

Stigmata Errata Etcetera by Bill Knott / Artwork by Star Black
Artist/Poet Collaboration Series Number Three

Ing Grish by John Yau / Artwork by Thomas Nozkowski
Artist/Poet Collaboration Series Number Two

Blackboards by Tomaz Salamun / Artwork by Metka Krasovec
Artist/Poet Collaboration Series Number One

Faulkner's Rosary was printed using the fonts Khaki and Electra.